Lord
I'm always smashing into a brick wall
In my battle with time and energy.
I want to serve You, dear God
But I'm not always sure of my mo-
tives. . . .

Dear child
Please leave something
for Me to do.

Lord, I Just Keep Running in Circles

RUTH HARMS CALKIN

LIVING BOOKS®
Tyndale House Publishers, Inc.
Wheaton, Illinois

Interior illustration by Marla Shega

Second printing, Living Books® edition, February 1989

Living Books is a registered trademark of Tyndale
House Publishers, Inc.

Library of Congress Catalog Card Number 88-50701
ISBN 0-8423-3828-4

CONTENTS

CONTENTS

Question
and
Answer

QUESTION AND ANSWER

O dear Lord
For so long I have been praying
Pleadingly, fervently
Day after wearisome day
Yet the heavens are as solid brass.
You have closed Your ears
To my desperate cry.
Why, Lord? Why?
Don't You love me anymore?

Dear wayward child
When will you understand
That praying
Is never a substitute
For obeying.

THE BATTLE

Lord
I'm always smashing into a brick wall
In my battle with time and energy.
I want to serve You, dear God
But I'm not always sure of my motives.
Am I fooling myself?
Is much of my dashing and rushing
A subconscious effort to impress?
How can I let myself relax and not feel guilty?
Over and over again I'm plagued
With deep emotional fatigue.
Should I ask for more physical energy?
I desperately need Your help, Lord.
How shall I sort my priorities?

Dear child
Please leave something
For Me to do.

YES OR NO?

Born of a Virgin . . .
Yes, Lord, I believe.
How could I dispute or debate
Your countless prophetic utterances
So accurately and amazingly fulfilled.

The Atonement . . .
Of course, Lord. I do believe
That when You died on the cross
You took my guilt
And poured into me Your righteousness.
It is a gift of grace.

The Resurrection . . .
Truly, it is forever settled
In my deepest heart
That You rose from the dead
And that this very day
You are at the Father's throne
Interceding for me.

My child
I do not ask for repetitious answers
To questions settled long ago.
I ask just one question now:
Will you trust Me with your life—
Yes or no?

NEVERTHELESS

Lord, right now
My life is one gigantic puzzle.
None of the pieces fit together.
None of them, Lord!
In my stupor and confusion
I confess I don't understand Your hand.

Nevertheless, My child
You can always trust My heart.

TWO QUESTIONS

O God
In my fear and frenzy
In my darkness and dread
My screaming question is
"Where *are* You?"

Wandering child
When things were going well
And you carelessly ignored Me
Where were you?

I WAS FURIOUS

This morning
A cantankerous neighbor said to me
"Not only do you drive as well
As your husband drives
But you can do it
On either side of the road!"
She laughed raucously as she said it
But I was furious, just furious!
Not only do I drive a little better
Than my husband drives
But I *never* drive
On the wrong side of the road.
Lord, could we move?

Child, could you forgive?

WHAT IS YOUR ANSWER?

O God, I call to You
But there is no answer.
I search for You
But I cannot find You.
I cry, but You do not come.
I hurt, but You do not help.
I reach for Your hand
But there is only empty space.
O God
Does it matter to You about me?
If Your answer is no
Just whisper it.
If it is yes
Please shout it!

I CAN SETTLE FOR THAT

The word *rebellion* frightens me.
I always associate it with
Revolt . . . terrorism . . . riots . . . death . . .
With economic and social issues . . .
With the drug scene
That promotes life without purpose.
I associate it with tempestuous waves of change
That leap up like wild animals.
Like the disciples in the storm
I want to awaken You, Lord.
I wonder why You seem to be sleeping.

But, Lord, maybe I don't
Really know You very well.
Maybe I don't let God be God.
After all, *You* are not frightened.
You do not hold Your hands up in despair.
You never say, "You should have come
    yesterday."
Nor do You say, "You're the wrong age and
    color."
You never say, "You're too timid, too slow."

You simply tell me to step out
Of my rocking boat.
You tell me to walk the waves with You.
You assure me You are not asleep.
You tell me to show genuine love
To a desperately needy world.

You insist it is far better
To walk over the billows than to go under them.
You tell me if I die in the attempt
At least I will die victoriously.
Then, facing me directly, You ask
"Can You settle for that?"
Lord, if You are with me
I can settle for that!

THE ANSWER

Lord, my life seems
So full of things
I can't do anything about.

True, dear child
But I will do something
With *those things.*

WITH EQUAL JOY

Lord, as I read Your Word
Morning after morning
May I say with singing heart
"Thank You, Lord
That this promise is for me."
When I come to Your commands
May I say with equal joy
"Yes, Lord, I will do them."

NO FURTHER

O God
So many things occur in my life
That are far, far beyond
My childlike comprehension.
My spirit is often bruised.
My thoughts are scattered.
I am left floundering and faltering.
There are shattering disappointments.
There are conflicts and doubts.
There are hours of emotional weariness.
And yet, the very thought
Of attempting to manage life without You
Brings more desolation
Than all other agonies packaged together.
I would rather endure the gigantic assaults
In Your Presence, dear God
Than live a single day
Without Your hand of protection.
For Your words to the Enemy of my soul
Are as powerful for me
As they were for Job:
"This far you may go, but no further."

URGENT REQUEST

Lord, You said in Your Word
I could talk to You
About anything—
Just *anything*, Lord.
So right at this precise moment
I have a very urgent request.
Will You please help me
Find my glasses soon enough
To remember why I needed them
In the first place?

WHY NOT START TODAY?

Lord, this lack of discipline
Has been going on long enough.
I just want to tell You
I'm sincerely going to watch
What I eat tomorrow.

Dear, weak child
Why not start today?

THE DECIDING FACTOR

Years ago
When I was still in high school
My wise and experienced father
Suggested four pertinent questions
Regarding each pending decision:

Will the result harm me?
Will it strengthen and build me?
Will it benefit others?
Will it please God?

Lord, I am confident
That neither I nor others
Would be harmed
But rather strengthened
If I answer yes
To the pending issue.
But, God, how can I know assuredly
That *You* will be pleased?

My child
Let my ruling peace
Be the deciding factor.

GOD, HOW CAN I DESCRIBE YOU?

O God
How can I describe You?
To whom can You be compared?
Your Word says
No one in all the world
Can begin to fathom
The depth of Your understanding.
You sit above the circles of the earth.
You stretch out the heavens like a curtain.
You count the stars
To see that none of them have strayed.
You pick up the islands
As though they had no weight at all.
So why should I grapple
With a single lingering doubt
That You are powerful enough to hold me?

MY "BEAUTIFUL THOUGHTS"

The other night at the dinner table
When our guests were sharing
Personal ideas and experiences
I watched carefully
For a break in the conversation
Which somehow never came.
I was especially eager
To share the "beautiful thoughts"
That had so inspired me
During my quiet time earlier that day.
At the end of the evening
After our guests had said good-night
I was pricked with slivers of guilt.
I wondered, Lord
What had been my greatest concern . . .
My unshared "beautiful thoughts"
Or the transforming power
Of Your Word itself?

THE QUESTION

Yes, Lord, I know.
This is the way it will always be.
When You give me a definite promise
It is never a question
Of what *You* will do.
It is always a question
Of what *I* will do.
Without a single doubt
You will always keep Your word.
The question is—
Will I believe You?

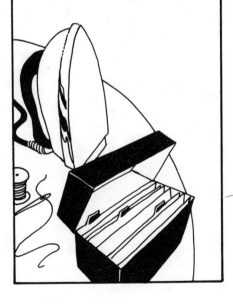

RUNNING IN CIRCLES

Lord
Why do I feel so uncertain?
I am always wondering
If I've made the right decision
Or said the right thing
Or planned the right guest menu
Or given the right advice.
I wonder if I've chosen the right dress
Or the right color of carpeting.
Often I ponder whether I should have
Taken on a certain responsibility.
When I make a phone call
I sometimes fear I will be misunderstood.
I wonder if I'm trying to do too much
Or if I should be doing more.
Sometimes I worry that I don't pray enough
Or read Your Word enough
Or witness enough.
Lord, I feel so utterly helpless.
What in the world is wrong with me?
Why am I always running in circles?

Troubled child
Nothing you could do
Would ever be "enough."
Just leave yourself alone
And delight in Me.

DESPERATION

O God
I am so sidetracked
So hard-pressed
From every direction.
I can't concentrate
I can't relax.
I feel like I'm going up
On a coming-down escalator.
There is grocery shopping to do
There are six phone calls to make
I must bake a birthday cake
And plan a party
And scrub the kitchen floor
And take my sick neighbor some soup
And pick up my husband's suit
And water the plants in the backyard
And clean the patio
And . . . O Lord, I'm simply desperate.
How can I handle it all
Without falling apart?

My frenzied child
I never ask of you
More than one thing
At a time.

HELP ME, DEAR LORD

Help me, dear Lord
Not to put off
Until tomorrow
What I know
I should never do at all.

WHEN I CANNOT UTTER A WORD

Because of a strange chemical imbalance
My husband has lost his ability to speak.
He can hear me
He can understand me
But despite his longing desire
He cannot verbally respond.
The doctor assures me
The puzzling malady will pass.
However, he is not sure how soon.
I sit by the hospital bed
To watch and wait—
To fervently pray.
I hold my husband's hand.
Gently, ever so gently
I tell him of my love.
Through the long, difficult hours
I continually reassure him.
He hears me, I know he hears me.
In his tired eyes I see his love.
But he cannot utter a word . . .
Not a single word.

O dear God
When my emotions are drained
When my heart is empty
When my hopes seem strewn on a dusty road
How well I remember
How gently *You* reassure *me*.
Even when I cannot utter a word . . .
Not a single word.

I JUST KEEP RUNNING IN CIRCLES

Often, Lord
I am too frantically busy
Getting nowhere fast.
I run, I rush
I grope for breath.
I start two new projects
Before finishing the last three.
I read but part of a book.
I reach for the broom
Before finishing the dusting.
In the middle of making a grocery list
I stop to make a telephone call.
It goes on and on like that
And then it gets worse!
I am like a seamstress busily sewing
Without a spool of thread on her machine.
Quiet me. Settle me. Establish me.
I'm so weary of running in circles.

TAKE MY HAND

Lord, take my hand
And help me up.
I long to stand tall and erect.
I long to breathe deeply, deeply
Of Your Presence.
Please rejuvenate me, Lord
With Your glorious strength
Until my amazed friends exclaim
"Look at you . . . just look at you!
You're standing steady and straight.
No longer are you weak and motionless."
With an explosion of gladness
I want to explain
"Jesus took my hand
And helped me up.
Now I shall walk by His side
For all of my life."
O Lord, I'm reaching out.
Take my hand
Help me up.

My child
Long, long
Before you were reaching toward Me
I was reaching toward you.
Here is My hand.
Now stand.

HIGH PEDESTAL

Lord, forgive me
For the times
I put myself
On a pedestal so high
That my husband
Can't reach me.
So often it is
When he needs me most.

MY HEART RAGES

O God, forgive me for saying it
But often my heart rages
Against the horrendous injustice
Of undeserved suffering.
The insidious ravages of war
The hunger-cries of starving children
The innocent victims of incurable diseases
The tragic accidents snuffing out life
In a moment of time . . .
Years of intense agony
Surgeries
Financial drain
Fears, tears, loneliness
Unbearable loss.
O God, do You hear me?
Often my heart rages
Against the injustice of it all.

My dear child
So does Mine.

THE DELIBERATE NO

O God, teach me to say
The deliberate and releasing word *no*
Without a spiritual tug-of-war
Between variations of false guilt.
May I say it tactfully
Kindly and gently
But enable me to *say* it!
If on occasions I am forced
To confront an honest doubt
May I wait patiently
For Your clear guidance.
May this powerful truth
Penetrate the inner chambers of my being:
It is better to say a God-guided no
Than a self-guided yes.
Lord, remind me often
That a squirrel cage
Can be mighty confining.
So can a heart attack
And a hospital bed.

STUDY TO BE QUIET

Lord, I'm completely burned out.
I haven't a drop of energy left.
I've got to start doing less
If I'm ever going to do more.
I must rest awhile
If I want to live awhile.
My deep desire is to serve You
But perhaps right now, dear Lord
I could do that best
In a quiet log cabin.
Lord, let's go to the mountains
For a few days . . . just the two of us
While You teach me
The meaning of Your admonition
"Study to be quiet."

THE END OF THE ROPE

O dear God
I feel as though I am clinging
To a rough, swinging rope.
Beneath me there is only emptiness.
My hands are bruised and bleeding.
There is no possible way
For me to tie a knot
At the end of the rope
And hang on.
O God, please help me.

Frightened child
Just let go.
I'll catch you.

LIVE BY THE MOMENT

O Lord
I am staggered by the enormity
Of the countless tasks
Flung at me today.
I simply don't know
How to tackle them all.
What shall I do first, Lord?
How shall I make room
For the interruptions
That are bound to come?
What shall I leave undone
When interruptions take priority?
Your Word clearly states
That You will guide me
With Your counsel.
You have promised Your wisdom
When my lack is so great.
I dare not plunge into the day
Without seeking Your guidance.
Lord, will You help me?

Anxious child
Live today
By the moment
Not by the year.

REACQUAINTED

Lord, please let me enjoy
A little private time
Just by myself today.
I feel so desperately the need
To get reacquainted with me.
For too long, *much* too long
I've been running in circles.

JUST BEGIN!

O dear God
How will I ever do it all?
I have so many hard tasks
I simply must get done today.
I'm exhausted just thinking about them.

My child
What you really have
Is an accumulation of easy tasks
You neglected to do yesterday . . .
And the day before . . .
And the day before.
I will help you.
Just begin!

RENEWED COMMITMENT

Forgive me, dear Lord
For too often
Letting the painful memories
Of my yesterdays
Crowd out the glad tomorrows
You graciously offer me.
I know I cannot rekindle
The charred embers
Of the past year.
I cannot erase the blunders
Made so impulsively
Nor can I regain the opportunities
That are forever lost.
I cannot retract the impetuous words
I wish I had not spoken
Or replace the shallow choices
I should not have made.
But I *can* open my wayward heart
To Your cleansing power.
With honest determination
I *can* renew my broken vows.
And I *can* begin to praise You
This very day
For the joy of beginning again.

SULLEN CHILD

Today I identify with Job
When he said he was reduced
To egg white without salt.
A great loneliness consumes me
As I walk through faded leaves
That seem anxious to die.
The hills are brown and barren.
Not a single creative thought
Grips or challenges me.
Someone crossing the street calls
"Have a happy day!"
I'm tempted to answer
"No thanks."
O God, what is wrong with me?
Why do I feel so dull?
Why am I so listless?
Why do You seem so distant
When I feel so alone?

Sullen child
Why don't you
Fill your days
With praise?

WHISTLING IN THE DARK

Lord
Today as I contemplate
A third surgery
So quickly following the second
It all seems so dark.
To be very honest
Even the thought of
Whistling in the dark
Has very little appeal.
I've never whistled well.
I wonder—
Could my guardian angel
Whistle for me?
Sorry, Lord.
When it comes right down to it
I really don't need a whistler—
Not even an angel.
I just need You.

UNEXPLAINABLE MYSTERY

Mysterious God
Today I am desolate
I am puzzled
I am heartsick
That I must wait so long
When You have promised so much.
At the same time
I am conscience-stricken
That I should feel such bitter rebellion.
Yet, to try to hide my emotions
Would only build up a pretense
That would eventually be exposed.
I suppose, O God
In the great perplexities
Of my unpredictable life
One of two things will always happen:
Either I will crowd You out
(Slowly but surely)
Or I will acknowledge Your sovereignty
In every area of my bewildered life.
To offer myself to You
Regardless of circumstances
May always bring unexplainable mystery.
But rejecting You totally
Brings the depth of despair.

THE PUZZLE

Lord, like the Apostle Paul
I don't understand myself at all.
The things I should do
I stubbornly rebel against doing.
The things I should not do
Are often deliciously tempting.
Why do I find it so hard to be good
And so easy to be bad?

Still
Growing

STILL GROWING

I love the words of the Apostle Paul:
"I haven't learned all I should even yet
But I keep working toward that day
When I will finally be
All that Christ wants me to be."

How this encourages me, Lord!
Paul knew and loved You so intimately.
He served You so faithfully.
Day and night he worked
To proclaim your reality.
He endured every kind of suffering
Willingly, gladly, for Your sake.
Yet, this very same Paul
Willingly confessed he hadn't arrived.
You were still "growing" him.
What was true for Paul is true for me.
My initial commitment took but a moment
My growth, dear Lord, will take a lifetime.
Thank You that You are responsible for both.

ONE REQUEST

God, I am determined to obey You
In what You have asked me to do
Even though at this moment I tremble
When I think of the possible consequences.
Nevertheless, should I choose
To ignore Your command
I fear even more the great personal loss
Disobedience eventually brings.
So, my Lord, I draw a deep breath
And deliberately step out
Into a seemingly reckless path.
I have but one request:
Please go before me and I will follow.

YOUR CHILD, GOD

O God
With deep contrition
I shamefully confess
My small concept of You
My puny faith
My limited comprehension.
Forgive me, O God
And enlarge my narrow vision.
Stimulate my trust
As I concentrate on Your greatness.
Give me even now
A true perspective
Of Your majestic power
To totally transform the child
On whom You have set Your love—
The child whose name is engraved
On the palm of Your hand
The child who claims You
As her Maker and Master.
Your child, God!
Me!

A GROWING MARRIAGE

Lord, we're still growing
In our marriage
And that's so good!
We're even doing better
When we criticize each other.
Like a gentle kitten
Courtesy is creeping in.
We feel the paws
Not the claws.

A BEAUTIFUL PLAN

Lord, on this first day of January
I've thought of a beautiful plan
For challenging the winter doldrums:
Once a week, dear Lord
I'll make a phone call
To a friend, or to an acquaintance
I've never called before.
Once a week I'll write a note
To our mailman, or to our doctor
Or to the boy who mows our lawn—
A note of deep appreciation.
Once a week I'll extend
A coffee invitation to someone
Who has never been in our home.
Once a week I'll try a new recipe
Or clean a kitchen cupboard
Or a storage shelf in the garage.
Once a week I'll read a recommended book.
And once a week I'll surprise my husband
With a tiny love gift—something just for him.
Lord, I do hope You're pleased with my plan.
Now please help me to do it
At least the first week!

BOUNDLESS LOVE

Lord, yesterday at the sunny beach
I traced crooked lines in the sand
With a small, damp twig.
The wet spray blew against my face
And a thousand thoughts
Went tumbling into the frolicking waves.
When I talked to You I heard You say
"My boundless love surrounds you."

Today I am at home again
Fixing meals, washing dishes
Talking on the phone, answering mail—
All the ordinary things, Lord.
When I talk to You I hear You say
"My boundless love surrounds you."
And dear God, suddenly I know
It is as true in my home today
As it was yesterday at the sunny beach!

EXCUSES

O God
I've become a self-educated master
Of a thousand polished excuses.
Hoping to avoid Your penetrating gaze
I clutch them to me like valuable gems.
When I think I have myself thoroughly covered
I'm caught short with the realization
That You see right through me.
My flimsy excuses are never really hidden.
I find an excuse for all my failures
Wrong choices
Late appointments
Wasted time.
I excuse my foolish blunders, my laziness
My broken resolves, my unreached goals.
I need Your help, Lord!
To hide from You is as foolish
As the Grand Canyon
Attempting to hide from the sky.
O God, my only hope
Lies in Your invincible power
To make me what I am not yet
But what You know I can become.
Strengthen my will, Lord.
Make me firm, steadfast, consistent.
Control my impulses, my emotions.
May I keep pursuing and never quit.

ON THIS VERY ORDINARY DAY

God, You don't always tell me
To do extraordinary, breathtaking things.
You simply tell me to let You
Make me an extraordinary Christian
In the ordinary, everyday walk of life.
So, dear Lord
On this very ordinary day
Will You make my life extraordinary
For Your purpose and for Your glory?

I PLEAD WITH YOU

Lord of my longing heart
I plead with You
To help me want *You*
More than I want *this*.
The unquenchable desire within
Is so overpowering, so consuming
At times I think
I can no longer endure it.
I think I would rather die
Than live without
That which so completely absorbs me.
And yet, dear God
There is the unwavering conviction
That what I want
Is not what You want for me.
There is the deep certainty
That the day would come
When my personal choice
Would close every future open door.
Lord, I cannot handle this alone.
I am not strong enough
Nor am I willing enough.
You alone can change my heart's desire.
You alone can make all things new.
O dear Lord, please help me
To want *You* more than I want *this*.

AS YOU HAVE FORGIVEN ME

Lord, all week long
I have struggled painfully
With the agony of unforgiveness.
In clinging to my hidden resentment
My spirit has been consumed.
Channels of creativity have been clogged.
I have been brittle, evasive, unyielding.
I've winced and wallowed in self-pity.
My health has been affected.
To pray has been a heavy burden.
I am starkly aware that I cannot afford
The luxury of an unforgiving heart
Unless I need no forgiveness from You.
There is no more room in my heart
For the twisting torment of this past week.
I am willing to drop the offense.
Now, dear Lord, please cleanse me.
Release me, purify me
And empower me to forgive
As freely as You have forgiven me.

THIS WAY AND THAT WAY

With solemn thoughtfulness
I read again today the story of Moses—
How he went to visit his fellow Hebrews
And saw an Egyptian knock a Hebrew down.
"Moses looked this way and that way
To be sure no one was watching.
Then he killed the Egyptian."
O Lord God
So often I am inclined
To look this way and that way . . .
This way and that way . . .
In the making of crucial decisions.
If only I would look steadfastly toward You
What tormenting grief, what inner turmoil
I would so often avoid!

THE CONCLUSION

Lord, Lord
I am not as brave
As You seem to think
Nor as strong
Nor as capable of standing firm
In the midst of affliction.
Lord, there is not a drop
Of emotional response in me.
No awareness of Your love
No comfort or joy in Your promises.
I have no deep conviction
That You are real.
There is no daylight in my heart
Nor even candlelight.
Nevertheless, with sheer determination
And perhaps a bit of spiritual grit
I have opted to throw my weight
On Your word *without*
Rather than my feelings *within*.
I don't know exactly when it happened
But I have reached the conclusion
That I would rather walk with You
In the dark of night
Than walk without You
In the light.

SUBMISSION

Dear God
When all my dreams shatter
When my plans go awry
When friendships cool
And neighbors annoy
Teach me to be submissive.
Enable me to say
As the Psalmist said
"O Lord, I adore you
As being in control of everything."

ONE OF TWO CHOICES

When You speak to me, Lord
I have one of two choices:
I either do what You say
Or I tell You I refuse to obey.
Perhaps that explains
My reluctance at times to listen.
Listening to You
Leaves one choice and an alternate.
And the choice is always mine.

TELLTALE SIGNS

I begin to see
All these little telltale signs
That remind me starkly
I'm no longer thirty years old—
Or even forty or fifty years old.
Last Christmas was a good example.
I prided myself on shopping early
But when it was time to wrap the gifts
I couldn't remember where I had hid them.
Please, dear Lord
Keep me smiling!
I have a strange feeling
It gets worse rather than better.

LESSONS IN PATIENCE

Dear Lord
After forty-three years of marriage
I think perhaps I've learned
A few practical lessons in patience.
For example, it isn't always easy
To laugh at my own jokes.
Especially when we have dinner guests
And my husband tells *my* jokes.

SO ASHAMED

I whimpered through my work this morning
As though I were the only one
In the entire world
With an ache or a pain.
Late this afternoon my sister called
To tell me she must once again
Face the dreaded trauma of chemotherapy.
Just a year ago her husband died.
As we talked she said
"I have been listening to tapes
Of his wonderful sermons
And I am so comforted . . .
So comforted . . ."
Lord, I remember my morning whimper
And I am so ashamed . . .
So ashamed.

I'M TEMPTED NOW AND THEN

Lord
I'm tempted now and then
To revert to spiritual immaturity . . .
To crawl into my highchair of rebellion
And beat my clenched fists
Upon the cold, plastic tray of self-pity.
But You have bigger plans
In mind for me, dear God.
You stand me straight on my feet
You scrub my stubborn heart
And send me on my way
To help another wailing child
Who desperately needs to grow.

LORD, I ADORE YOU

O dear Lord, I adore You!
With my whole heart
I joyfully praise You
For Your incredible goodness to me.
Above all else
I praise You for *You*.
Like Mary who sat at Your feet
I love You extravagantly.
My deepest longing
Is to exalt Your name.
Work in me Your good pleasure
And may I bring great glory
To Your Father—and mine.

A WATERED GARDEN

O dear God
I don't want to be
A plastic flower
Without life
Without fragrance
Without growth.
I want to be real!
Transplant me if You must.
Root me, cultivate me
Water me, weed me.
Send the rain
Send the sun
Until I am like a watered garden
Delighting the heart of my God!

YOUR WAY, LORD

Lord, in no way do I claim the right
To "program" my own life.
Nor do I want to feed my own
Unmanageable impulses.
I am not asking today
For time to do this or that.
I simply ask for renewed energy
To do joyfully and willingly
Whatever You want me to do
In the time You give me to do it.

SETTLED DECISION

God, it is my settled decision
Not to choose less
When You have chosen more for me.
Not to choose the worst
When You have chosen the best.
Not to stoop to defeat
When You have provided victory.
Not to let my emptiness
Close the door to Your fullness.

COMMUNICATION BREAKDOWN

How subtle it is, God—
The breakdown of communication
Between husbands and wives . . .
Between members of a family.
It doesn't come like a sudden cyclone
Sweeping away words and deep feelings.
Rather, it starts with little jabs
Little rivalries, little revolts.
It starts with blaming each other
Until aloofness develops.
Dialogue becomes monologue
And there is no freshness anymore.
There is no transparency.
Lord, in our family
We need to hear each other.
We need to catch each other's smiles.
We need to listen, to share, to care.
We need to learn when to start talking
And when to say nothing.
Often we need to keep giving
Until something breaks.
Then we need to keep on giving
Until something heals.
Lord, when it comes right down to it
We're just Your little kids
And we need to grow up.
Help us, God. Please help us.
We really love each other
But we've been in nursery school
Much too long!

Reaching Out

TRIBUTE

Lord, how can I adequately thank You
For a husband whose commitment
Remains solid and steadfast
Through forty-three years of marriage?
How can I thank You for his reassuring smile?
His sound judgments?
His wise counsel?
Through the cumulative years
He has so often fortified my faith.
With gentle understanding
He has reestablished my wavering values.
When the fogs of life
Have been unusually dense
He has stood faithfully by my side.
When I've been caught in the tangles
Of anxiety and stress
He has helped me put things together again.
He has brought gigantic joy into my life.
And always, Lord
He is my reason for wanting to hurry home.

TAKE JOY

I see them on skateboards
As they skate by our yellow house.
I see baseballs and bats
And transistor radios
Strapped securely to shoulders.
I see bright sweatshirts
And worn shoes, and crazy hats.
I see a little guy with a red wagon
Who stoops to examine a parade of ants.
Then, with a small twig
He casually pushes the ants aside.
His faithful mongrel watches and waits.
I hear squeals of laughter
And hilarious comments.

It's Saturday! No school!
A day of freedom, a day for fun.
Freedom to ride, to run, to hike.
Freedom to explore new trails
To breathe the fragrance of spring.
Freedom to drink in the warmth of the sun.
I'm happy . . . happy for *their* happiness.
I remember similar Saturdays of long ago
And the exhilarating sense of freedom.
But suddenly I remember, too
How transitory happiness is.
So quickly it can be brushed aside
By corroding circumstances.

I long to call, to shout:
"Hey, kids, listen!
Take a minute and listen.
Open your young hearts to *joy* . . .
The joy that comes from God alone.
It's so different from happiness.
It's real, it's permanent.
Nothing can destroy it:
Neither tears nor pain nor tragedy.
Whatever else you may lose
In the shuffle of life
Joy you may keep forever.
Hey, kids, listen!
Take God's word for it.
It's His personal gift.
His Son made it possible.
You'll never regret it.
I know! I know!
Take joy!"

A MAN OF TALENTS

Lord, You've blessed my husband
With an amazing amount of talent.
He can do so many things well.
I love to listen to his deep, rich voice
When he sings a solo.
I love to watch him direct a huge choir.
I love the way he paints commercial signs.
When he leads a Bible study
I am always amazed at his fresh insights.
He makes our yard look like a beautiful park.
However, I've made one interesting discovery:
With a few tools in his hand
In no time at all
The dripping faucet in our kitchen
Becomes a rushing stream.

THE GREATEST NEED

Lord, how can I help this woman
Who is coming to have tea with me today?
She wants to discuss her personal problems
But I find it difficult to talk to her.
Trying to get a word in edgewise
Is like trying to thread a sewing machine
With the motor running.
She says she simply has no time
To get everything done.
She bemoans the fact
That she's always running in circles.
But when I try to make suggestions
About managing her time
She stands up vigorously in her own defense
And falls down miserably on her priorities.
I'm sorry, Lord
But I really feel she does me more harm
Than I do her good.

Dear child
Just listen to her.
She needs that most.

EXPENSIVE QUESTIONS

Again today my husband told me
How thoroughly he enjoys his work
As assistant to the chaplain
In the Christian therapy unit
Of a psychiatric hospital.
Then he said with a twinkle in his eye,
"I'm glad I'm not a patient there.
The psychiatrists at the hospital
Ask a lot of expensive questions
That you ask me for nothing!"
I wonder, Lord . . .
Do I need to guard my tongue
More carefully?

AUTHENTIC

Lord, thank You
For my authentic friend
Who is so obsessed with You
That her Sunday morning smile
Always holds over
Through Saturday night.

A WALKING GIANT

In stature he was a very little boy
And today he is a very little man.
Spiritually, however
He is a walking giant.
Every time I see him
He seems to have grown
By leaps and bounds.
"You amaze me"
I said to him one day.
"How do you explain your spiritual growth?
Do you have some private secret?"
"No secret." He smiled.
"It's just the nourishment I take.
I eat the Bread of Life
I drink Living Water
And I continually feed on God's Word."
Just a little man he is.
Perhaps as tall as Nicodemus was.
But he never climbs a tree
In order to see over a crowd.
He'd rather look up than down.
From his tall heart
He has a magnificent view of heaven.

FRUSTRATED DESIRES

All day long, dear Lord
Her haunting words
Have swept through my aching heart.
"Frustrated desires . . ."
Together we stood at the card rack
Looking at birthday cards.
Wanting to be friendly
I said nonchalantly
"It's difficult to choose
When they're all so beautiful."
She looked toward me pensively.
"My husband died three months ago.
We always gave each other
Beautiful cards.
Today is his birthday.
I wish I could give him
The whole rack."
Pushing back the tears
She said half-apologetically
"I'm sorry, I didn't mean
To trouble you
With my frustrated desires."

I cannot comfort her, Lord.
I don't even know her name.
She left the store so quickly.
But not for a single moment
Is she lost to You.
Wherever she is right now

Hold her close to Your loving heart.
Comfort her, quiet her, dear God
And transform her frustrated desires
Into happy, heart-shaped memories
Until she is able to say
With trust and confidence
"Nothing can separate me
From the love of God."

PRAYER FOR A HUSBAND

Lord, on this first day of the new year
I pray for my husband—
Your dearest love-gift to me.
May he enjoy vibrant health
And a sense of deep satisfaction
In the work You've chosen for him.
Enlarge his vision.
Give him full knowledge of Your will.
Keep him calm and objective
In every difficult situation.
Fulfill his high expectations, Lord.
Encourage and uphold him.
Above all, give him, I pray
A very personal relationship with You.
I claim for him Your promise to Abraham:
"I will bless you
And you shall be a blessing."
Lord, what more could I ask
For the husband who is more than life to me?

THE SEARCH

There is scarcely a day
That she does not argue with someone.
If it is not with her husband
It is with her mother
Or with her husband's mother.
Often she argues with her children.
Again and again she argues with friends.
When she grocery shops
She argues over prices and brands.
Sometimes I think her tirades
Are sort of a challenge
To see how long she'll be withstood.
But somehow in her arguments
I hear overtones of deep yearnings.
She seems to be seeking a way
Out of her personal dungeon.
Yet she is afraid of the light.
I wonder, dear God . . .
Is her greatest battle with herself?
Or is her most crucial argument with You?
God, I long for her to experience
Your liberating power
But when she begins to argue
We come to a standstill.
I am at a loss to know how to help her.

Dear child
Share your victories
But confess your defeats.

Share the light
But confess that there are shadows.
When she knows she is not alone
Her desperation will subside
And her search for Me will begin.

THE CONTRAST

Without any doubt, Lord
He's an excellent professor.
But I had a difficult time
With this today:
His shining eloquence
In the classroom
And his shameful etiquette
In the dining hall.

HALLOWEEN NIGHT

Halloween night . . .
Winds tingling . . . air cool and crisp
Goodies stacked near the door
Porch light blazing . . .
Squeals of laughter
Ghosts, clowns, Mickey Mouse
Indians, ballet dancers . . .
Seven-fifteen . . . eight-thirty
A few late stragglers
Finally a chance to eat our dinner.

Then a sort of shuffling sound
The doorbell again.
He stood there alone
A gruesome mask covering his face
So small, so young.
I knelt down to face him directly.
With mock seriousness, I said
"You really scare me!
I'd better close the door—quick!"
He lifted the corner of his mask.
"Do you want to see how I *really* look?"
I saw twinkly brown eyes
A freckled nose
A please-love-me grin.
We hugged each other—hard.

O God
In this crowded world of many masks

Please forgive my lack of compassion.
Remove my own pretenses
Until I see *persons*
Created in Your image
For Your divine purpose.
Above all, dear God
Make me a channel of Your *unmasked* love.

GRANDFATHER

He never headed a great corporation.
He was not a college president
Or an author or a financier.
His academic education concluded
In a shabby red schoolhouse
With a potbellied stove.
Every Sunday morning, rain or shine
He sat in the same pew
Of a tall-steepled country church.
If anyone had asked him to repeat
The main points of a sermon
He could not have done it
Had his life depended on it.
At the end of the service
He cautiously felt his way
Down the narrow aisle
To shake an outstretched hand
Or to rumple a tousled head.
When someone suggested he teach a class
He declined with a hearty laugh:
"I don't know too much theology—
Most of my learnin' is Doxology!"
But how he extolled You, dear God.
What honor he brought to Your name!
His grandson said it beautifully:
"He was a walking demonstration
Of a man who lived for God."

THE GAIN IS ALL THEIRS

O dear God
How they must love heaven—
My precious parents
Who made earth so rich
While they were here.
This very day
They laugh with fullness of joy
Run with fullness of energy
Serve with fullness of commitment
And praise with fullness of exaltation.

Never again need they
Ponder or analyze.
Never again need they
Ask Your forgiveness.
Never again need they sense
The slightest disappointment
Or question the wisdom
Of their decisions.
Singing without sorrow
Gladness without gloom
Delight without despair!
O dear God
The pain is on our side
The gain is all theirs.

GIFT EXCHANGE

She is so lonely
So at loose ends with herself
A sorry picture of dejection.
I had hoped to encourage her when I said
"To some God gives the gift of marriage
To others the gift of *not* being married."
She pushed back a strand of blonde hair
And asked ruefully
"Have you ever been given a gift
That you wanted to exchange?"
I didn't quite know how to answer her.
Lord, what should I have said?

STARK REALITY

He is forty-two years old.
All his erratic life
He has been making feeble excuses
For his wasted years
His lack of discipline
His refusal to accept responsibility.
Yesterday he said
With exaggerated gestures
"Remember the old proverb
'Eat, drink, and be merry
For tomorrow we die'?"

But, Lord
The stark reality is this:
In all probability
Tomorrow he will *not* die.
Tomorrow . . . and tomorrow
He will look back
And remember.

FUTURE MATES

Right now, dear Lord
Somewhere in this giant world
There is a young boy
For whom You have
A unique and special plan.
He may be pulling a wagon
Or fishing by a stream
Or stuffing cookies into his pocket.
His eyes are blue or gray or brown
His hair—is it light or dark?
It doesn't really matter.
It only matters that You hold him close
As he learns to walk with You.
As he grows to be Your man
Give him wisdom from above.
Give him singleness of mind
And purity of heart.
May he set worthy goals
And dream big dreams.
Wherever he is, Lord
Keep him strong and safe
Until in Your own good time
In Your own incredible way
You bring them together
To love, honor, and cherish—
The precious newborn daughter
Who lives next door to us
And the boy who is known to You.

EMPOWER HER TODAY

Lord, despite what she tells me
Of her unquenchable love
For the husband of the other woman
She is cheating herself so terribly.
She is putting a million-dollar investment
Into a ten-cent ride.
She is like a little child
Who purchases a dime-store diamond
Giddily pretending it's the real thing.

How will she explain your unchanging values
To her own lovely daughter
Who will soon be twelve?
How will she guide her
In the swift approaching years
When *she* must work through temptation?
How will she protect her
Against the fiery emotions
That entangle so rapidly?

Purity is not a harsh, hissing word.
Purity is Your word, Lord.
O God, burn within my confused friend
The inescapable truth
That "free" love is never free . . .
That physical intimacy will disintegrate
Unless it serves Your plan and purpose . . .
That she cannot break Your commands

Without breaking something immeasurably
   sacred
Within her own God-planned life.

Lord, she is Your child.
A hundred times she has said
"If only I knew the right way."
Deep in her homesick heart she does know.
Empower her to walk it—*today.*

A NEW SUIT

Lord, I want to talk to You
About a very personal matter.
Perhaps You will smile—
But why is it so difficult
To persuade my husband
To shop for a new suit?
He *needs* a new suit.
He can *afford* a new suit.
I'll gladly shop with him
When he can be persuaded to go.
It's not that he flatly refuses—
He just keeps putting it off.
"Maybe next week," he said this morning.
It's the twinkle in his eye
That finally dissolves my exasperation.
A friend told me to be grateful.
"After all," she said
"When a husband has but one suit
He can always find his car keys."
Frankly, I hadn't thought of that.
So when the day finally comes
That we take the great plunge
We'll visit the locksmith, too.
Lord, Your Word specifically says
You changed the mind of a king.
So please hear my request
And change my husband's mind, too.

"I WANT TO GET RICH"

I asked, "What do you plan to do
When you finish college next month?"
He stood with his hands in his pockets.
Tall, suntanned, grinning contageously
"You're not going to like this, maybe—
But to tell you the truth I want to make money.
I just want to get rich!"
Another college graduate out to get rich.
If only he knew, dear God
That in You he is already rich.
How said that he refuses to yield his life
And accept his great wealth.

OFF-TRACK LIFE

God, though she is only in college
Already she is steeped in fear
And shattered with guilt.
With aching agony
She longs for inner peace.
I find it difficult
To know how to help her
In her bewilderment
And self-condemnation.
Nevertheless, I have promised
To stand by her side
Through the pitch-black tunnel
Of her off-track life.
But in the darkness, dear God
May I gently remind her
That I cannot give her light.
You alone can do that.

The Gift

THE GIFT

Lord
The shopping is finished
The gifts, beautifully wrapped
Are placed with gentleness
Under our smiling tree.
We chose carefully, Lord
Just the right gifts
For those who are so dear to us.

Today I am suddenly aware
That long years ago
In the fullness of time
You sent the Gift of Your Son
Because we are so dear to You!
O God, thank You!

TAKE MORE

Lord God
How can I adequately express
My overwhelming gratitude
For all Your amazing goodness?
When I kneel to thank You
Your answer is always the same:
Take more!

On this Thanksgiving morning
I give myself anew to You.
Take more of me, dear Lord—
Take more!

TINY PACKAGE

O God
What a tiny package
You sent at Christmas time
To reveal such a
Priceless Treasure.

CUP OF JOY

Lord, forgive me
For drinking out of
My saucer today.
You see, I really
Have no choice
Since You've made
My cup of joy
So overflowing.

SMALL BIT OF HEAVEN

Make me, dear Lord
A small bit of heaven
In a sick and frenzied world
So seemingly intent
On destroying itself.

SALT AND STARDUST

Lord, through the years
We are learning
That marriage is a combination
Of salt and stardust—
Salt for hamburgers
And stardust for poetry.
Undoubtedly we could survive
A little longer on hamburgers
Than we could on poetry.
But why should we settle for one
When we know You want us to have both?

CONFESSION

O God
You are the Creator
Of light and darkness
Sun and rain
Summer and winter
Streams and desert
Great and small.
You give laughter and tears
Victory and trials.
And yet, I frankly confess
I find it painfully difficult
To praise You equally
For laughter *and* tears.

OPEN THE BOX

Dear God
Perhaps what I read is true:
"There is no problem without a gift in it."
But I am so perplexed, so confused
So incredibly weary
I haven't sufficient energy
To untie the ribbon and open the box.
My Lord, will You please do it for me?

THE FAMILY OF GOD

In the family of God
We need not pretend to be
What we know we are not.
In the family of God
Our acceptance is not based
Upon how superbly we perform.
Our material possessions
Or lack of them
Are of little consequence.
Our personal failures
Do not shatter our relationships.
In the family of God
We are free to express
Our longing desires
Our loneliness, our fears
Our deep-seated frustrations.
In the family of God
We can freely acknowledge our needs
And expect the loving response
Of family members.
In the family of God
There is forgiveness
There is faith, there is hope
There is joy, there is love.
At least, dear God
This is Your desire
For the family You dearly love.

THE SERMON

I love what our pastor said
In his helpful sermon
This bright Sunday morning:
"The gospel is not
Third-class mail marked Occupant.
It's first-class mail marked Personal."
Once again, dear Lord
I gleaned a fresh glimpse
Of Your very personal love
For me.

A SONG OF PRAISE

O God
Thank You for the sheer pleasure
Of waking up to a newborn day.
There is no possible way to know
What each day will bring. . . .
Some days are warm and sunny.
Others are damp and overcast.
Often I awake to the sound of rain
Falling steadily on our roof.
There are days when a gentle wind
Hugs our sleepy house.
Some days I feel the chill
Of an early frost.
Other days the mountains
Are freshly blanketed with clean snow.
But just to put my feet on the floor
To stretch, to yawn, to breathe deeply
To pull back the drapes
And greet the dawn with a song—
What a challenge, what a gift!
Again today, dear Lord
I lift my joyful heart in praise
For Your marvelous treasure called *day*.

A TENDER KISS

I was walking alone
Under rain-filled clouds
When suddenly I felt
The tender kiss of a raindrop.
Lord, it almost felt
Like a kiss from You!

FOR BETTER, FOR WORSE

Lord, over forty years ago
We made a solemn promise:
"For better or for worse."
Today we are stumbling through "worse."
Though our emotions are a bewildered mixture
Of agony and love, please quiet us, Lord.
Free us from the desire to retaliate.
Above all, help us both to remember
We are as bound to our promise today
As we were yesterday
When we basked in the sunlight of "better."
Even now, dear Lord
Help us to make it better again
By not putting off what we both know
We must eventually do
If healing is to take place.
The simple but beautiful word is forgiveness.

WOULDN'T YOU RATHER?

Lord God
You can as easily
Send blue skies
As heavy clouds.
Because You are a happy God
Wouldn't You rather?
Today, dear God.
Today!

NEITHER LONELY NOR BLIND

Lord God
May I never cling to fantasies
Or create illusive dreams
That will leave me longing
For the things I don't have
Or blind to the abundance of good
You have already given me.

JUST A BAD DAY

The wind was rebellious yesterday.
Twisting, shouting, screaming, stomping
Like a spoiled child.
I was angry inside.
I don't know why exactly.
My husband said
"You are like the wind."
Sorry, Lord.
It was just a bad day.
Today the sky is clear
And the sun shines brightly.
I'm feeling much better.
I hope when my husband comes home
He'll say, "Hi, Sunshine!"

At
Long
Last

AT LONG LAST

O Lord
At long last
I have placed in Your hands
The strong and aching desire
Which for so many months
Completely absorbed me.
Now to my surprise and delight
I have made the joyful discovery
That all my tenacious resistance
Was far more painful, more agonizing
Than a total letting go
In obedience to Your command.

My child
So it will always be.

ENORMOUS REWARDS

O dear God
Thank You for teaching me
The enormous rewards
Of walking obediently with You:
There is joy without guilt
Freedom without fear
Satisfaction without sordidness
Purpose without confusion
Friendship without compromise
Forgiveness without penance
Fulfillment without disappointment.

CRUCIAL DAY

God, how well I remember
The crucial day
I asked You to create within me
A heart of deep compassion—
Even if it could be accomplished
Only through some great anguish.
How sweepingly, how painfully
You took me at my word.

CRUCIAL DECISION

Lord, today I must make
A very crucial decision.
The decision will ultimately
Affect every area of my life—
Not only now, but in the years to come.
In my deepest heart I am convinced
That nothing is ever truly settled
Until it is settled right.
And nothing is ever settled right
Until it is settled with You.
God, You know my personal limitations
And my desperate need for Your help.
Please superimpose Your thoughts on my mind
And grant me the peaceful assurance
That I am following Your guidance.
I am so aware that the decision I make today
Will be inherited by those I love—tomorrow.

AFTER ALL, THERE IS GOD

She came for her piano lesson
With a big chunk of news for me.
She was going to have tonsil surgery.
Naturally we had to talk about it.
I asked, "Are you scared, Susie?"
Only a moment's pause.
"Not very. Just a tiny bit scared."
"You're very brave, Susie.
I'd probably be very frightened."
Her flashing smile put the sun to shame.
"No, you wouldn't. After all, there *is* God."

O God, Susie is right!
Whatever the emergencies, the anxieties
The twistings and turnings
The crushing sorrows
There is God.
To trust You in the darkest night
Simply because of who You are
Because You are good
Because You are in control—
This is the secret of serenity.
God, make it *real* in my life
Not just something I read in a book.
May I give You the joy
Of total confidence in You.

SONGS OF CELEBRATION

With overflowing gratitude
The Psalmist said
"We will write songs
To celebrate Your mighty acts!"
Lord, on the keyboard
Of my grateful heart
I too have composed many songs
To celebrate Your unequaled greatness
Your faithfulness
Your splendor and majesty.
Lord, the most triumphant song of all
Exalts Your measureless love.
With joy and adoration
I sing it again and again.
As long as I live, O God
I shall continue to sing
My songs of exuberant praise!

THE GLORY OF GOD

Dear God
Too often my spoken words
Are sadly inconsistent
With my unspoken thoughts.
Too often my prayers for purity
Are inconsistent with my deliberate wrongs.
Too often my expressed resolves
Are inconsistent with my hidden faults.

The Psalmist said so magnificently
"The heavens are telling the glory of God . . .
Without a sound or word
Their message reaches out
To all the world."
God of all creation, recreate me.
Restore my wayward heart.
Blot out all sham and shame.
Day and night
Without a sound or word
May the purity of my life
Display the glory of God.
Wherever You place me
May the message reach out
To all the world.

MY HEART'S DESIRE

O dear God
What joy, what tremendous exaltation
King David must have experienced
When he said to You triumphantly
"How the king rejoices
In Your strength, O Lord!
For You have given him his heart's desire—
Everything he asked You for!"
Now, dear God
Please hear my request as You heard David's.
With my whole heart
I want *from* Your
Everything You want *for* me.
Then I too shall be able to say
"You have given me my heart's desire—
Everything I asked You for!"

ALL NIGHT LONG

Lord, thank You!
All night long I stayed awake with You.
We shared the hours together
From nine o'clock until early dawn.
I wasn't disturbed or anxious.
I just felt wonderfully close
To Your loving heart.
My husband slept.
My family slept.
As far as I know, my neighbors slept.
But You and I were awake, dear Lord.
I told You my intimate longings
My deepest desires.
Even my gross failures, Lord—
The ones I was so reluctant to confess.
And You shared shining secrets with me.
Secrets that will, I trust
Make me a more obedient child.
Your Word says so clearly
You neither slumber nor sleep.
I wonder . . . did You enjoy my company
As much as I enjoyed Yours?
Oh, Lord, I hope so!
For me it was a night I'll never forget.

I WAIT FOR YOU

O God
I have waited so long
Under dark clouds of trial and testing
And yet Your promise is clear and precise:
"Blessed are all those that wait for Him."
Though I see no glimmer of hope
Though my tears come unbidden
I am still waiting
For the clouds of trial
To break into refreshing showers of blessing.
Because You have promised, dear Lord
Surely my waiting cannot be in vain.
I wait for You . . . I wait for You . . . I wait.

THE BIRDS ARE BACK

This morning at the breakfast table
A full flock of birds
Descended on our front lawn
Singing their hearts out!
In his prayer my husband said
"Lord, how we thank You
That the birds are back!"
At that moment I thought of the trauma
Of the mysterious past year.
Heartache, disappointment, pain
Despair, death, change.
Then I remembered Paul's wonderful words:
"Nevertheless afterward . . ."
With a glad heart I too rejoice
That the birds are back.
On this beautiful spring morning
I am singing with them.

FOR SO LONG

For so long, dear Lord
I have tried to fit You
Into my personal plans.
I've tried to crowd You in, somehow
Between my own chosen priorities.
Now at long last
I ask You to fit *me* into *Your* plans.
Mold me, teach me, use me
In whatever way will honor You.
O dear Lord
Give Yourself a magnificent reputation
In my God-planned life.

A VALUABLE LESSON

Thank You, Lord
For teaching us a valuable lesson
In our search for the pot of gold
At the end of the rainbow.
We've learned to pick up
A little silver here and there
Along the rugged way.
It's the silver that helps us
Pay our bills on time each month.

HOLD ME CLOSE

A little while ago
I said to my husband
"You're very quiet tonight—
You've spoken only a few words.
Is everything all right?"
"Everything is fine," he said.
"I really don't think
We need a lot of words.
I just want to hold you close."

Lord, sometimes
When You seem so silent
Is it that way with You?
Do You just want to hold me close?
If so, forgive me
For flinging my whys
And begging for explanations.
Forgive me for complaining about delays.
Help me just to quietly rest
In the shelter of Your arms
While You hold me close.

INDESCRIBABLE JOY

O God, thank You!
Today I learned
With indescribable joy
That one solid hour
Of drastic obedience
To Your command
Is a thousand times
More rewarding
Than months of frantic shouting
"Tomorrow, Lord
Tomorrow . . . tomorrow."

WHEREVER I LOOK

Lord, wherever I look I see spring!
Pansies and yellow daffodils
Border the green lawns
All over our neighborhood.
The graceful trees are branching
In every direction.
Shining leaves are eagerly
Getting acquainted with each other.
The password this morning is Joy.
Joy laughing and singing
And chasing sunbeams all over the hills.
To me it seems to have happened overnight.
Yet I know You have been quietly preparing it
For many long months.
Lord, help me to wait patiently
For "spring" in my life
When the winter months seem endlessly long.

HEAVEN'S JOY

Lord, sometimes I think
The dearest thing about heaven
Is just these few words:
"Where I am there you may be also."

Other Living Books® Best-sellers

THE ANGEL OF HIS PRESENCE by Grace Livingston Hill. This book captures the romance of John Wentworth Stanley and a beautiful young woman whose influence causes John to reevaluate his well-laid plans for the future. 07-0047 $2.95.

ANSWERS by Josh McDowell and Don Stewart. In a question-and-answer format, the authors tackle sixty-five of the most-asked questions about the Bible, God, Jesus Christ, miracles, other religions, and creation. 07-0021 $3.95.

THE BEST CHRISTMAS PAGEANT EVER by Barbara Robinson. A delightfully wild and funny story about what happens to a Christmas program when the "Horrible Herdman" brothers and sisters are miscast in the roles of the biblical Christmas story characters. 07-0137 $2.50.

BUILDING YOUR SELF-IMAGE by Josh McDowell. Here are practical answers to help you overcome your fears, anxieties, and lack of self-confidence. Learn how God's higher image of who you are can take root in your heart and mind. 07-1395 $3.95.

THE CHILD WITHIN by Mari Hanes. The author shares insights she gained from God's Word during her own pregnancy. She identifies areas of stress, offers concrete data about the birth process, and points to God's sure promises that he will "gently lead those that are with young." 07-0219 $2.95.

COME BEFORE WINTER AND SHARE MY HOPE by Charles R. Swindoll. A collection of brief vignettes offering hope and the assurance that adversity and despair are temporary setbacks we can overcome! 07-0477 $5.95.

DARE TO DISCIPLINE by James Dobson. A straightforward, plainly written discussion about building and maintaining parent/child relationships based upon love, respect, authority, and ultimate loyalty to God. 07-0522 $3.50.

DAVID AND BATHSHEBA by Roberta Kells Dorr. This novel combines solid biblical and historical research with suspenseful storytelling about men and women locked in the eternal struggle for power, governed by appetites they wrestle to control. 07-0618 $4.95.

FOR MEN ONLY edited by J. Allan Petersen. This book deals with topics of concern to every man: the business world, marriage, fathering, spiritual goals, and problems of living as a Christian in a secular world. 07-0892 $3.95.

FOR WOMEN ONLY by Evelyn and J. Allan Petersen. Balanced, entertaining, diversified treatment of all the aspects of womanhood. 07-0897 $4.95.

400 WAYS TO SAY I LOVE YOU by Alice Chapin. Perhaps the flame of love has almost died in your marriage. Maybe you have a good marriage that just needs a little "spark." Here is a book especially for the woman who wants to rekindle the flame of romance in her marriage; who wants creative, practical, useful ideas to show the man in her life that she cares. 07-0919 $2.95.

Other Living Books® Best-sellers

GIVERS, TAKERS, AND OTHER KINDS OF LOVERS by Josh McDowell and Paul Lewis. This book bypasses vague generalities about love and sex and gets right to the basic questions: Whatever happened to sexual freedom? What's true love like? Do men respond differently than women? If you're looking for straight answers about God's plan for love and sexuality, this book was written for you. 07-1031 $2.95.

HINDS' FEET ON HIGH PLACES by Hannah Hurnard. A classic allegory of a journey toward faith that has sold more than a million copies! 07-1429 $3.95.

HOW TO BE HAPPY THOUGH MARRIED by Tim LaHaye. One of America's most successful marriage counselors gives practical, proven advice for marital happiness. 07-1499 $3.50.

JOHN, SON OF THUNDER by Ellen Gunderson Traylor. In this saga of adventure, romance, and discovery, travel with John—the disciple whom Jesus loved—down desert paths, through the courts of the Holy City, to the foot of the cross. Journey with him from his luxury as a privileged son of Israel to the bitter hardship of his exile on Patmos. 07-1903 $4.95.

LIFE IS TREMENDOUS! by Charlie "Tremendous" Jones. Believing that enthusiasm makes the difference, Jones shows how anyone can be happy, involved, relevant, productive, healthy, and secure in the midst of a high-pressure, commercialized society. 07-2184 $2.95.

LOOKING FOR LOVE IN ALL THE WRONG PLACES by Joe White. Using wisdom gained from many talks with young people, White steers teens in the right direction to find love and fulfillment in a personal relationship with God. 07-3825 $3.95.

LORD, COULD YOU HURRY A LITTLE? by Ruth Harms Calkin. These prayer-poems from the heart of a godly woman trace the inner workings of the heart, following the rhythms of the day and the seasons of the year with expectation and love. 07-3816 $2.95.

LORD, I KEEP RUNNING BACK TO YOU by Ruth Harms Calkin. In prayer-poems tinged with wonder, joy, humanness, and questioning, the author speaks for all of us who are groping and learning together what it means to be God's child. 07-3819 $3.50.

MORE THAN A CARPENTER by Josh McDowell. A hard-hitting book for people who are skeptical about Jesus' deity, his resurrection, and his claims on their lives. 07-4552 $2.95.

MOUNTAINS OF SPICES by Hannah Hurnard. Here is an allegory comparing the nine spices mentioned in the Song of Solomon to the nine fruits of the Spirit. A story of the glory of surrender by the author of *HINDS' FEET ON HIGH PLACES*. 07-4611 $3.95.

NOW IS YOUR TIME TO WIN by Dave Dean. In this true-life story, Dean shares how he locked into seven principles that enabled him to bounce back from failure to success. Read about successful men and women—from sports and entertainment celebrities to the ordinary people next door—and discover how you too can bounce back from failure to success! 07-4727 $2.95.